A Heath

Cooking, Baking & Brewing

By
Craig Brooks
&
Emma Brooks

For Ocean Runa Pearl Brooks

Introduction 11

Spring 15

Cheesy Asparagus & Bacon Tart 16

Salmon Gravlax 17

Vegetable Noodle Soup 18

Lamb & Mint Meatballs 19

Vegetable Lasagne 20

Elderflower & Gooseberry Fool 21

Banana Muffins 22

Summer 27

Cod topped with Oats 28

Pea & Mint Soup 29

Gammon cooked in Mead 30

Spaghetti Bolognese 31

Mushroom & Spinach Carbonara 32

Lemon Curd Cake 33

Vegan Chilli Chocolate Brownies 34

Autumn... **39**

Mushroom Pasta... 40

Prawn & Potato Curry..41

Rissoles 42

Toad in the Hole 43

Butternut Squash Soup... 44

Apple & Mead Cake...45

Bread Pudding 46

Winter **51**

Pork and Barley Stew...52

Sausage Casserole 53

Vegetable Stew...54

Fish Pie..55

Nut Roast 56

12 Mini Fruit Cakes.. 58

Apple and Blackberry Whiskey Crumble 60

Campfire cooking 65

Beany Chilli 66

Fennel, Courgette & Chicken Kebabs 67

Lamb Rogan Josh 68

Spicy Tomato Pasta.. 69

Chilli, Ginger & Lime Mackerel Fillets 70

Chocolate Banana Melt.................................... 71

Damper on a Stick 72

Breakfasts 77

Raspberry and Honey Pancakes 78

Spicy Scrambled Eggs.................................... 79

Mush 80

Garlic Mushrooms 81

Kedgeree 82

Bread 87

Sourdough Starter 88

Chocolate Rye Bread.. 89

Rosemary Sourdough 91

Black bread 93

Garlic Sourdough Flatbreads............................95

Garlic Baguettes.. 96

Everyday Loaf 98

Jams & Preserves 105

Lemon Curd 106

Fiery Ginger Marmalade 107

Crab Apple Jelly...108

Blackberry Jam 109

Damson Jelly 110

Rhubarb & Vanilla Jam 111

Sweet Chilli Jam 112

Chutney... 113

Mulled Pears 114

Pickled Beets 115

Alcoholic Drinks 121

First Steps 122

Mead 124

Parsnip Wine 125

Ginger Wine 126

Elderberry and Blackberry Wine.................127

Elderflower Champagne - make with caution! 128

Sloe Gin..129

Idiot Mead...130

Rosemary and Bay Beer............................. 131

Pumpkin Beer 132

Nettle Beer 133

Non-alcoholic drinks...139

Elderflower Cordial....................................140

Drivers Mead 141

No Mojo Mojito.......................................142

Further Reading 147

Fire he needs, who with frozen knees
has come without;
food and clothes, must the farer have,
the man from the mountains come.

Introduction

The original idea for this book was to write recipes based on Norse and Anglo-Saxon cooking, which we would have failed at; Other books, by people who actually know what they are talking about, have already been written, and the general consensus from historians is that day-to-day meals were probably based on savoury porridge and not much else.

What we do know is that our ancestors had to fend for themselves-skills in foraging, baking, brewing and preserving aren't essential now, but they are still fun to learn. Again, better books by better people are available on all of those subjects, but we'd like to give a taste of how easy these things can be, and get you started with the basics. A list of more in-depth books that we use at home is at the back.

Our hope is that we can encourage you to think more about your food. These skills can also offer ways for you to contribute to your communities, through gift ideas and inspiration for hosting your own celebrations and events.

Giving something you've made to family, friends, and guests, is a great way to connect with other people; home-made offerings can be a great way to connect with nature and the land around you; and exploring the history behind recipes can be a great way to connect with your ancestors.

If you can enjoy sitting round a fire, sharing music, mythology, knowledge and mead, you'll be living well- and if you can bring some home-brew or some good food you'll be helping other people to enjoy it too.

- Emma Brooks 2017

During the writing process, we've come to realise that it's not just our ancient ancestors whose recipes have been lost, but also our more recent ancestors too. My mum is not around for me to ask, so I have to recreate things as best I can, and now that we have a family of our own, we create our own family meals and traditions.

Some things evoke powerful memories, like the moment we hear a certain song, or smell a certain thing. Food is no different. Certain foods instantly bring images back, like my grandad giving toast rubbed with garlic to my mum, despite, or perhaps, in spite of, my dad's hate of garlic.

We have included some space at the end of each section of this book to add your own family recipes, before they are lost to time. I often hear people say "my mum/nan made the best...." - Only no one thought to write them down.

We would like to encourage you to take this opportunity whilst you can, then share it with us on the Facebook group 'A heathen guide to...', where we'd like to build a community based on swapping and preserving recipes.

With thanks to:

Jardar Nygard, Kari Marie Heland, Daniel Serra and Luke Molony for your inputs on historical meals.

Bob Thornton and Chris Butcher for inputs on recipes.

James Collins, Jophis Laybourne and Rich Blackett for helping try out recipes.

Thanks to Rich Blackett for asking me to write the book and to everyone who has ever tasted my homebrew or food and given me feedback.

- Craig Brooks 2017

Skål!

I rede thee, Loddfafnir! and hear thou my rede,
profit thou hast if thou hearest,
great thy gain if thou learnest:
if a friend thou hast whom thou fully wilt trust,
then fare to find him oft;
for brambles grow and waving grass
on the rarely trodden road.

Spring

First snowdrops, then skylarks, then frogspawn - spring seems to turn up in the same weekend.

Some heathens celebrate the Easter/Eostra feast on the spring equinox, some on the nearest full moon, some wait for the flowers to bloom; at home, we like to celebrate the first round of planting. Time for lighter meals with fresh sweet peas and salads, and time to find a good spot for foraging baby nettles.

Cheesy Asparagus & Bacon Tart

This one is a bit of a cheat! It's quick to put together, but really tasty. I make it with pre-rolled puff pastry, but you could make the pastry from scratch.

Serves 2

Ingredients:

- 320g Pre-rolled puff pastry
- 250g Streaky bacon (cut into 2cm pieces)
- 1 fennel bulb (cut into small pieces)
- 1 leek (cut into small pieces)
- 1 garlic clove (crushed)
- Salt and pepper
- Olive oil
- 100g asparagus sticks
- A little Cheddar cheese to top

Method:

Heat the oven to 220 degrees

Place the pastry onto a baking tray and fold the sides in, to form an edge. Place baking beads onto the pastry and put into the oven for about 10 minutes to brown.

Meanwhile fry the fennel, leek and garlic in a little olive oil, with the bacon. Season with salt and pepper.

Take the pastry out of the oven, remove the baking beads and cover with the vegetables and bacon. Trim and lay the asparagus sticks across the top and cover with slices of cheese, I use cheddar, but mozzarella would work well.

Place in the oven for 5 - 10 minutes until the cheese has melted and started to brown.

<u>Salmon Gravlax</u>

This is a very famous Old Norse dish, a traditional Method to preserve fish that has become expensive to buy. Traditionally this would have been fermented, and some recipes add vodka or gin.

Serves 4 as a starter or light lunch

Ingredients:

- 80g granulated sugar
- 80g sea salt
- 20g dill (finely chopped)
- Juice of a lemon
- Pepper (to season)
- 2 salmon fillets

Method:

Mix the sugar, salt, dill & lemon juice well and season with pepper.

Place some cling film into a dish and lay 1 salmon fillet, skin side down and cover with the sugar/salt mix.

Place the second fillet, skin side up, on top and wrap tightly in the cling film.

Place something heavy on top and leave in the fridge for 2 - 4 days, depending on how salty you want the fish to be. Turn every 12 hours.

When ready, drain liquid and slice thinly.

Serve on rye bread.

Vegetable Noodle Soup

As spicy as you need it to be, this is a perfect comfort food for a rainy day.

Serves 2

Ingredients:

- Olive oil
- Pinch of chilli flakes
- Thumb sized piece of ginger (peeled and grated)
- 1 garlic clove (grated)
- 4 spring onions (chopped)
- 300g Udon noodles
- 1 tablespoon Chinese rice wine
- 1 tablespoon soy sauce
- 1 vegetable stock cube
- 100g broccoli (chopped) (purple sprouting broccoli if you can get it)
- 100g asparagus (chopped)
- 1 handful of sugar snap peas
- 1handful of fresh coriander (finely chopped)

Method:

Fry the chilli, ginger, garlic and spring onions in a large saucepan for several minutes.

Add the rest of the ingredients except the coriander and cover with boiled water.

Simmer for 5 minutes and serve topped with the chopped coriander.

Lamb & Mint Meatballs

This is lighter than the traditional springtime roast lamb, with mint, one of the easiest herbs to grow and the first to pop up again after the winter.

Serve with salad or noodles

Serves 2

Ingredients:

- 500g lamb mince
- 4 handfuls of fresh mint (finely chopped)
- Tablespoon of honey
- 1 egg
- Salt & Pepper
- Olive oil

Method:

Stick all the ingredients into a bowl, season with the salt & pepper, and mix well.

Squish the mixture together to form small balls. You are aiming for about 16. If the balls are too big, they may burn before cooking through, due to the honey.

Heat some olive oil in a frying pan. Add the meatballs and cook on a low heat for about 10 minutes, turning occasionally, until cooked through.

Vegetable Lasagne

I rarely make a lasagne with meat, I don't think you really need it. A good dish for when we have visitors, it always goes down well, even with hard-core carnivores.

Serve with a fresh salad and buttered garlic baguette.

Serves 4

Ingredients:

- Olive oil
- 1 onion (peeled and ends trimmed)
- 1 green pepper (top, seeds & pith removed)
- 100g Purple sprouting broccoli (ends trimmed)
- 1 leek (ends trimmed)
- 2 cloves of garlic (grated)
- 1 tin chopped tomatoes
- 2 tbsp. tomato puree
- 2 tsp Oregano
- Salt & pepper
- Lasagne pasta
- Jar of lasagne cheese sauce
- Cheddar cheese (to top)

Method:

Put the onion, pepper, broccoli & leek into a food processor and blitz. You are aiming for a mince-type consistency, with no big lumps.

Add oil and vegetables in a saucepan. Fry for several minutes. Add the garlic, tomatoes, puree and oregano. Season and bring to the boil, and cook for about 5 minutes.

Grease a baking dish and add a layer of vegetables sauce, followed by a layer of pasta, cheese sauce, more pasta, vegetables sauce, and so on. Finish up on a cheese sauce layer and top with grated cheddar.

Cook in the centre of a pre-heated oven at 220 degrees for about 25 minutes until golden on top.

Elderflower & Gooseberry Fool

Elderflowers announce the coming of summer. You can find them growing almost everywhere. The bulk of the bush is poisonous, containing cyanide, but the flowers and the berries are perfectly safe to eat.

They complement the tartness of the gooseberry, which happens to ripen at just the same time.

Serves 4

Ingredients:

- 6 elderflower heads
- 300g gooseberries
- 3 tablespoons of caster sugar
- 200ml double cream

Method:

Heat the elderflowers, gooseberries, and sugar, in a pan, with a splash of water. Simmer for 10 minutes, until the gooseberries start to break up.

Rub through a sieve into a bowl.

Whip the cream to soft peaks and fold into the gooseberry and elderflower puree.

Divide into glasses and chill for a couple of hours before serving.

Banana Muffins

This recipe is perfect for using up those slightly sweeter, over ripe, bananas.

Makes 12 muffins

Ingredients:

280g plain flour (sieved)

1 tsp bicarb pre-heated

Pinch of salt

3 large bananas (mashed)

125g honey

1 egg (beaten)

80ml mead

40ml olive oil

40g linseed

Pumpkin seeds (to top)

Method:

In a large bowl mix the bananas, honey, eggs, oil & mead.

Add the flour, bicarb, and salt, and mix well. It should still be quite lumpy. Add the linseeds and stir through.

Divide the mix into cupcake cases and sprinkle a few pumpkin seeds onto each one.

Put in the centre if a pre-heated oven for 20-25 minutes at 180 degrees

Recipe

Ingredients:

Method:

Recipe

Ingredients:

Method:

Recipe _____

Ingredients:

Method:

I rede thee, Loddfafnir! and hear thou my rede,
profit thou hast if thou hearest,
great thy gain if thou learnest:
a good man find to hold to friendship,
and give heed to his healing charms.

Summer

Crowds descend on Stonehenge and the wheat stands tall in the fields, if it doesn't get squished by the crop-circle makers; We enjoy midsummer and then look forward to the only heathen festival in the UK, the Asgardian, at the end of July.

Time for barbecues, berries, and too many courgettes.

Cod topped with Oats

Traditionally, oats were a staple part of living, with savoury porridges being a large part of the diet.

Here, the oats are used to give a crunchy topping to cod, but this would work with any white fish, or even stronger fish, like mackerel.

Serve on a bed of spinach with garlic flat breads.

Serves 2

Ingredients:

- 2 Cod fillets
- Rolled oats
- 2 tsp English mustard
- Salt and pepper
- Olive oil

Method:

Drizzle a frying pan with olive oil and place your cod skin side down into the pan.

Coat the top of the cod with the mustard and drizzle with a little more oil. Add a pinch of salt and pepper.

Sprinkle a layer of oats over the cod and gently press down.

Fry on a low heat for about 5 minutes. Carefully turn the fish and cook for a further 5 minutes, until cooked through.

Pea & Mint Soup

This might be the easiest fresh meal you'll ever make. Ideal for those warm summer days when the last thing you want to do is be in the kitchen.

Delicious hot or cold. Serve with crusty sourdough bread.

Serves 2

Ingredients:

- 300g peas (frozen or fresh)
- 1 leek (chopped)
- 1 garlic clove (crushed)
- 2 large handfuls of fresh mint leaves
- 850ml vegetable stock
- Salt and pepper to taste

Method:

Put all the ingredients into a pan and simmer for 10 mins.

Blitz well with a hand blender and refrigerate for a couple of hours, if eating chilled, or eat straight away.

Gammon cooked in Mead

I had the idea to try this one for myself, after my Sister-in-law's fiancée cooked us a gammon in cola. I then found out that Bob Thornton of MoreMead had already done it; Here's his recipe.

Ingredients:

- Gammon
- Mustard
- Cloves
- Bottle of mead

Method:

Soak the gammon in water for a couple hours to remove excess salt.

Place the gammon in a pan and cover with mead, bring to the boil and simmer for a couple of hours. Top up the liquid with mead or water, if necessary, to keep the gammon fully covered.

Pour away the liquid and let the gammon cool a little.

Heat the oven to 180. place the gammon into a roasting tin, remove the rind and score the fat.

Mix a little mead with some mustard and coat the gammon all over with it. Stud with cloves.

Roast in the oven for 30 mins.

Spaghetti Bolognese

This one has a special place in our family, as it was the last meal we all had together, just a few days before my mum died.

Serve with spaghetti and buttered garlic baguettes.

Serves 4

Ingredients:

- Olive oil
- 1 onion (chopped)
- 500g beef mince
- 2 carrots (chopped)
- 2 celery sticks (chopped)
- 10 mushrooms (sliced)
- 2 garlic cloves (grated)
- 1 tin chopped tomatoes
- Handful of basil (finely chopped)
- 2 tbsp. tomato purée
- 1 stock cube
- 125ml red wine
- 10 cherry tomatoes, (cut in half)
- Salt & pepper (to taste)
- Cheddar (grated for topping)

Method:

Heat a little oil in a large pan, on a low heat. Add the onions and cook for a few minutes. Add the mince and cook for 3 - 4 minutes until the meat is browning.

Add the rest of the ingredients to the pan and stir well. Increase the heat. Bring to the boil and simmer for about 40 - 45 minutes, stirring occasionally until the sauce thickens up.

Mushroom & Spinach Carbonara

A vegetarian twist on a classic carbonara.

Serves 4

Ingredients:

- 400 g tagliatelle
- Olive oil
- 150g chestnut mushrooms (sliced)
- 1 clove garlic (grated)
- Large handful of spinach leaves
- 1 tsp fresh chives (finely chopped)
- 1 tsp fresh parsley (finely chopped)
- 2 eggs
- 100g single cream
- 50g grated Parmesan (grated)
- Small handful pine nuts
- salt & pepper

Method:

Put the tagliatelle on to cook, following the packet instructions.

Heat some olive oil in a pan and add the mushrooms & garlic. Fry on a low heat for about 5 minutes. Add the spinach.

Beat the eggs, with the single cream and parmesan and stir in the chives and parsley.

Add the mushrooms and spinach and season with salt and pepper.

Drain the pasta and, off the heat, stir in the sauce and pine nuts.

<u>Lemon Curd Cake</u>

This recipe is quick to put together as long as you have lemon curd; You could use shop bought, but for a little extra effort you could make some- head to the preserves section of the book to find out how.

Ingredients:

- 140g self-raising flour
- 110g caster sugar
- 110g butter (room temp)
- 2 eggs, beaten
- 2 heaped tablespoons lemon curd
- For topping:
- Honey
- Juice of half a lemon

Method:

Heat the oven to 170 degrees.

Put all the ingredients into a bowl and mix well with an electric mixer.

Grease and line a 2lb loaf tin and add your cake mixture.

Place in the centre of the oven and cook for about 1 - 1 ¼ hours. If it browns too quickly place some greaseproof paper over the top.

Remove from the cake tin and squeeze over the lemon juice and drizzle with honey.

Vegan Chilli Chocolate Brownies

Chilli and chocolate is one of my favourite combinations. If you are into spicy things you can up the amount of chilli to your taste.

You can use the juice from a can of chickpeas, or any legume, as an egg substitute. It goes by the name of Aquafaba.

In this instance, the brownie works better with Aquafaba, rather than egg, making a stickier brownie.

Ingredients:

- 300g really dark chocolate
- 300g light soft brown sugar
- 250g vegetable spread (I use Stork)
- 1 teaspoon of chilli flakes
- 220g plain flour (sifted)
- the water from 1 can of chickpeas

Method:

Preheat your oven to 180 degrees.

Put the chocolate, sugar, spread, and chilli into a pan and slowly heat until dissolved.

Meanwhile whisk the chickpea water to form soft peaks.

Take the chocolate mix off the heat and stir in the flour. Fold in half the chickpea water followed by the other half.

Pour into a baking tray or cake tin and cook for around 20-25 minutes.

Recipe _____

Ingredients:

Method:

Recipe _____

Ingredients:

Method:

Recipe _____

Ingredients:

Method:

I rede thee, Loddfafnir! and hear thou my rede,
profit thou hast if thou hearest,
great thy gain if thou learnest:
be never the first to break with thy friend
the bond that holds you both;
care eats the heart if thou canst not speak
to another all thy thought.

Autumn

Golden leaves, darkening days, a chill in the air - all the lovely clichés of autumn have arrived. Festivals often start with the equinox, then move on to Winter Nights, often including the pagan Samhain as well as Halloween. Time for pickling, harvesting, and leftover Haribo

.

Mushroom Pasta

We're not fans of mushrooms, but we wanted a good vegetarian recipe for the autumn. I found a version of this and it looked very tasty, so thought I'd give it a go. I made a rule that if it goes in the book, I have to have at least made and tasted it myself. Long story short, we now like mushrooms!

It would be possible to make this using any kind of mushrooms, so perhaps, if you know what to look for, you could forage some. I'd suggest 'chicken of the woods' as a good starting point.

Serves 2

Ingredients:

- 250g Orzo pasta
- Olive oil
- 250g chestnut mushrooms (sliced)
- 1 leak (chopped)
- 2 garlic cloves (grated)
- 1 teaspoon of thyme (finely chopped)
- 1 teaspoon of balsamic vinegar
- 3 tablespoons of mead
- 2 handful of Kale
- Salt & Pepper (to season)

Method:

Cook the orzo, following the instructions on the packet.

Meanwhile, heat some olive oil in a large frying pan. Add the mushrooms and cook for 5 minutes, on a low heat, tossing occasionally.

Add the leek, garlic, thyme, balsamic vinegar and mead, and cook for a few minutes until most of the liquid has gone.

Drain the pasta and stir in the mushrooms. Add the kale, mix thoroughly and season with salt & pepper.

Prawn & Potato Curry

This is one of my favourite curries. It takes little effort to make, but has an amazing flavour. It's great served with homemade garlic flatbread or rice.

Serves 2

Ingredients:

- Olive oil
- 1 onion (chopped)
- 2 garlic cloves (grated)
- Thumb sized piece of ginger (peeled and grated)
- 1 green pepper (chopped)
- 500g potatoes (chopped into chunks)
- Can of chopped tomatoes
- Pinch of chilli flakes
- ¼ tsp of Cumin seed
- ¼ tsp turmeric
- ¼ tsp ground coriander
- ¼ tsp paprika
- ¼ tsp cayenne pepper
- Salt & pepper
- 180g king prawns
- Fresh coriander leaves (to garnish)

Method:

Put the potatoes on to boil for about 10 minutes.

Heat some oil in a large saucepan, add the onions, garlic & ginger and cook for 2 or 3 minutes to soften.

Add the pepper, potatoes, tomatoes & spices. Season to taste and simmer for around 5 minutes. Add the prawns and cook for a further 3 or 4 minutes until pink.

Serve topped with fresh coriander.

Rissoles

Thanks to my grandad, these will be forever known in my family as arseholes. I love them, though they don't seem to be that well known in the UK. There are many different versions available, but this is how I remember them from my childhood.

Serve with boiled potatoes and gravy.

Serves 2

Ingredients:

- 1 onion
- 250g lamb mince
- 40g breadcrumbs + a little extra for coating
- $1/4$ teaspoon cinnamon
- Handful finely chopped parsley
- 1 garlic clove (grated)
- Salt & pepper to taste

Method:

Blitz the onion in a food processor. Add all the ingredients to a bowl and mix well.

Split the mixture into 4. Squash each portion firmly into a ball shape and flatten each ball to form a burger.

Put some breadcrumbs onto a plate and push the rissoles into the crumbs, coating all the edges and sides.

Heat some olive oil in a large frying pan and cook the rissoles for about 5 minute on each side.

Toad in the Hole

A classic British recipe. At home, we usually use pork sausages when we cannot get hold of decent quality toads.

Serve with mash potato, fried onions & gravy.

Serves 4

Ingredients:

- 12 chipolatas
- Olive oil
- 140g plain flour (sifted)
- ½ tsp salt
- 2 eggs
- 175ml semi-skimmed milk

Method:

Heat the oven to 200 degrees.

Grease a roasting tin and add the sausages. Put into the oven for about 10-15 minutes, turning occasionally, until brown.

Meanwhile, put the flour and salt into a jug with the eggs and slowly add the milk whilst whisking.

When the sausages are nice and brown take them out of the oven and pour the batter over them.

Put back into the oven for about another 30 minutes, until the batter is risen and golden in colour.

<u>Butternut Squash Soup</u>

Warming and slightly spiced, this squash recipe should get you in the autumn mood.

Serve with crusty sourdough bread.

Serves 2

Ingredients:

- 1 small squash (chopped into small chunks)
- 4 small sweet potatoes (peeled and chopped)
- 1 vegetable stock
- $\frac{1}{2}$ a teaspoon of cinnamon
- $\frac{1}{2}$ a teaspoon of nutmeg
- 1 bay leaf
- Salt & pepper (to taste)

Method:

Add all the ingredients to a pan and cover with water. Bring to the boil and simmer for around 10 minutes until the squash and potatoes are soft.

Remove the bay leaf and discard. Blitz the rest of the ingredients with a hand blender and serve.

Apple & Mead Cake

This pudding is inspired by a German apple cake, replacing the milk and sugar to make a really moist honey flavoured cake.

Every autumn I prune my neighbour's apple tree in exchange for buckets of fresh apples and this pudding is perfect for using them up.

Ingredients:

- 125g vegetable spread, I use stork
- 160g honey
- 2 eggs
- 225g plain flour (sifted)
- 1 level tsp baking powder (sifted)
- ½ tsp salt
- 70 ml mead
- ½ a dessert apple, sliced into thin wedges
- 1 ½ tsp of demerara sugar
- ½ tsp of cinnamon

Method:

Preheat the oven to 180 degrees.

Beat the spread, honey and eggs together in a bowl with an electric mixer.

Add the flour, baking powder, salt & mead. Mix well.

Spoon into a 7½ inch round cake tin and arrange the apple slices in a circle on top of the cake. Mix the sugar and cinnamon and sprinkle over the top of the cake mix.

Wrap the tin in greaseproof paper, this will help prevent the cake from burning.

Cook for 40 - 45 minutes in the centre of the oven.

Remove the paper for the last 5 minutes to allow the top to brown a little.

Drizzle with a little honey and leave to cool for 15 minutes before slicing. The cake will continue to cook during this time.

Bread Pudding

I grew up eating this, when I could get some- my nan used to make a big bread pudding and cut it in half for my grandad and dad but they never liked to share it; Now I make the pudding, and share a slice over a cup of tea.

This is great for using up stale bread. Store small amounts of bread in the freezer until you have enough for a pudding.

Traditionally the 'liquid' would be milk, but due to Emma's dairy allergy, I usually use a fruity wine, but you could use almond milk. To be honest, any liquid should work. I have used beer, and have heard of people using whisky.

Ingredients:

- 800g bread (torn into pieces)
- 1kg mixed dried fruit
- 2 tbsp. ground mixed spice
- ½ teaspoon of cinnamon
- ½ a teaspoon of ground ginger
- 600ml liquid
- 2 large eggs
- 250g dark Muscovado sugar
- zest and juice of a lemon
- 100g vegetable spread. I use Stork (melted)

Method:

Put everything except the spread into a large bowl and scrunch it up, to completely break up the bread, and mix it up well.

Add the melted spread and mix well again.

Grease and line a large baking dish and pour in the mixture. Sprinkle with a little sugar. Cover with foil or baking paper to stop it from burning.

Place in the centre of a pre-heated oven at 170 degrees for about an hour and a half until firm and golden. Remove the foil/paper for the last 15 mins to allow the top to brown a little.

Recipe

Ingredients:

Method:

Recipe_____

Ingredients:

Method:

Recipe _____

Ingredients:

Method:

I rede thee, Loddfafnir! and hear thou my rede,
profit thou hast if thou hearest,
great thy gain if thou learnest:
exchange of words with a witless ape
thou must not ever make.
For thou mayst from an evil man
a good requital get
but a good man oft the greatest love
through words of praise will win thee.

Winter

Fat on mince pies and tipsy on mulled wine, winter is perfect for having fun in the kitchen when it's too cold to go outside. Yule, or midwinter, is probably the most popular heathen festival, often encompassing the solstice, mother's night (Modraniht), and Christmas. In some parts of Britain, a wassail, usually in January, is good way to round off the party season. Time for thick stews and rich fruit cake.

Pork and Barley Stew

This winter stew is great for using up the last of the garden veg. The pearl barley makes for a hearty meal.

Serve with crusty bread, such as the rosemary sourdough in the bread recipes section of this book.

Serves 2

Ingredients:

- 300g pork shoulder (diced)
- 200ml cider
- 200g pearl barley (rinsed)
- 1 carrot (sliced)
- 1 leek (sliced)
- A handful of kale
- 1 stock cube
- ½ tsp black mustard seeds
- 1 sprig of rosemary (finely chopped)
- Salt & pepper (to taste)

Method:

Stick all the ingredients into a large pan and cover with water.

Bring to the boil and simmer uncovered for about an hour, until the meat is tender and the stew has thickened. Don't let the stew run dry, and add a drop more water if necessary.

Sausage Casserole

This is inspired by the food we ate at Midgardsblot festival in Norway. Don't be put off by the pickled beets and courgettes, they give a great flavour to the stew without being overpowering.

Serve with crusty bread.

Serves 2

Ingredients:

- Olive oil
- 12 chipolata sausages
- 1 tsp mustard seeds
- 2 garlic cloves (grated)
- 1 leek (chopped)
- 1 fennel bulb (cut into smallish cubes)
- Large handful of kale (chopped)
- Handful of pickled beetroot (cut into smallish cubes)
- 10 slices of pickled courgette
- 6 mushrooms (sliced)
- ½ a bottle of mead
- 500ml chicken stock
- Salt & pepper to taste

Method:

Put some olive oil into a casserole dish and add the sausages and mustard seeds. Cook on the hob, on a low heat, for about 5 minutes, turning occasionally.

Add the garlic, leek and fennel and fry for a couple of minutes. Add half of the mead and cook for a few minutes.

Add the kale, pickled beets, courgette and mushrooms, the rest of the mead and stock. Season with salt and pepper. Stir well.

Pop a lid on the dish and cook in the centre of a pre-heated oven at 180 degrees for 45 minutes.

Vegetable Stew

This recipe is given as an example; it should be a way of using up any leftover vegetables you have in the cupboard.

Serves 2

Ingredients:

- 1 small turnip (chopped into chunks)
- 2 carrots (sliced)
- 2 parsnips (sliced)
- 2 handfuls of Kale
- 1 leek (sliced)
- 1 Vegetable stock cube
- 350ml white wine (I use parsnip)
- 1 tablespoon Rosemary (finely chopped)
- 1 tablespoon Thyme (finely chopped)
- 1 tablespoon Sage (finely chopped)
- Salt & Pepper (to taste)
- Dumplings:
- 100g vegetable suet
- 200g self-raising flour (sieved)
- 1 tablespoon Rosemary (finely chopped)
- 200ml cold water
- Salt & Pepper (to taste)

Method:

Stick all the ingredients into a large pan and add enough water to cover. Bring to the boil and simmer for about an hour until reduced and thickened.

Add all the dry dumpling ingredients to a bowl and slowly add the water whilst mixing with your hands, until it all comes together. You may need slightly more or less water than stated.

Divide the dough into 8 – 10 and press firmly into balls. Carefully drop them one at a time into the stew and simmer for about 20 minutes.

Fish Pie

Can't think of much to say about this one, other than yum!

Serves 4

Ingredients:

- 800g potatoes (peeled and chopped)
- 400g fish pie mix
- 1 carrot (grated)
- 1 parsnip (grated)
- Handful of kale (chopped)
- 10 cherry tomatoes (halved)
- 1 garlic clove (grated)
- 1 tsp fennel seeds
- 1 lemon (juice and rind)
- Small handful of parsley (finely chopped)
- Olive oil
- Salt and pepper
- Cheese (grated)

Method:

Put the potatoes on to boil for 10-15 minutes, until soft.

Meanwhile put the carrot, parsnip, kale, cherry tomatoes, garlic, fennel seeds, lemon juice and rind, fish and parsley into a deep dish and mix well. Drizzle with olive oil.

Drain the potatoes, drizzle with olive oil and season with salt & pepper. Mash well.

Spread the mash evenly over the top of the fish/veg mix and top with cheese.

Cook in the middle of a preheated oven at 200 degrees for about 40 minutes until golden on top and cooked through.

Nut Roast

This is a traditional Sunday roast alternative- just as time consuming to make, but tasty and super healthy.

Serves 4

Ingredients:

- 1 tablespoon olive oil
- 1 large onion (finely chopped)
- 2 sticks celery (finely chopped)
- 2 garlic cloves (finely chopped)
- 200g chestnut mushrooms (finely chopped)
- 1 red pepper (deseeded and finely chopped)
- 1 large carrot (grated)
- 1 tsp dried oregano
- 1 tsp smoked paprika
- 100g red lentils
- 2 tbsp. tomato purée
- 300ml vegetable stock
- 100g breadcrumbs
- 150g chestnuts (chopped)
- 80g dried cranberries
- 6 tablespoons Aquafaba (juice from a can of chick peas)
- 1 handful flat leaf parsley (finely chopped)
- Salt & pepper

Method:

Heat the oil in a large pan and cook the onion and celery for about 5 mins, to soften. Add the garlic and mushrooms and cook for a further 10 mins.

Add the red pepper, carrot, cranberries, oregano and paprika and cook for a few minutes.

Add the red lentils, tomato puree, and the vegetable stock and simmer over a very gentle heat until all the liquid has been absorbed and the mixture is fairly dry.

Stir in the breadcrumbs, nuts, Aquafaba, parsley, and season with salt & pepper.

Spoon the mixture into a greased and lined 2lb loaf tin and press down the surface. Cover with foil and bake in a preheated oven at 180 degrees for 20 mins, remove the foil and bake for a further 10–15 mins until firm.

12 Mini Fruit Cakes

I usually make this in September and feed it every couple of weeks, up till December, with a mixture of brandy, dark rum, and sloe gin, for a really boozy cake.

You'll also need 12 small (and empty) 'half tins' of baked beans.

I like to make these as gifts, covered in icing and marzipan.

Ingredients:

- 1kg mixed dried fruit
- 50g chopped glacé cherries
- Brandy
- Kraken rum
- Sloe gin
- 225g plain flour (sifted)
- ½ teaspoon salt
- ¼ level teaspoon nutmeg, freshly grated
- ½ level teaspoon ground mixed spice
- 225g dark brown soft sugar
- 4 large eggs
- 1 dessertspoon black treacle
- 225g vegetable spread
- 50g chopped almonds
- zest of 1 lemon and 1 orange

Method:

Put the dried fruit into a bowl and add 100ml of brandy. Mix well and cover the bowl with a cloth. Leave to soak overnight.

pre-heat the oven to 140°C

Put the flour, salt, spices, sugar, eggs, treacle, and spread, into a large bowl and beat with an electric hand whisk until thoroughly mixed.

Fold in the pre-soaked fruit mixture, chopped nuts and finally the grated lemon and orange zest.

Grease and line the tins and spoon the mixture evenly between them.

Wrap the tins in a double layer of greaseproof paper, covering the tops of the cakes.

Bake on the lowest shelf of the oven for 60-90 minutes until they feel springy to the touch.

Leave to cool before removing from the tins and skewering all over and feeding with a small drop of rum.

Wrap in greaseproof paper and store somewhere cool and dry. Feed every 2 weeks.

If you want to decorate the cake with marzipan and icing, do this shortly before eating.

Apple and Blackberry Whiskey Crumble

I don't like to waste things, so this is a great way of using up left over blackberries, once you have made blackberry whisky.

(See the sloe gin recipe in the Alcoholic drinks section for how to make blackberry whiskey)

You could use normal blackberries or apples. In fact, you could experiment with just about any fruit.

Ingredients:

- For the crumble;
- 225g plain flour
- 60g light brown sugar
- 125g of oats
- 175g unsalted butter (room temperature)
- For the fruit:
- 800g apples (peeled, cored and diced)
- 30g unsalted butter
- 150g light brown sugar
- 350g blackberries (left over from making blackberry whiskey)

Method:

To make the crumble put the flour, oats and sugar into a bowl and rub in the butter. Alternatively, stick it in a food processor until mixed through and crumbly.

To make the fruit base, heat the butter and sugar in a pan until melted together. Add the fruit and mix well.

Put the fruit into a baking dish and cover with the crumble mix. Cook in the middle of a pre-heated oven at 190 degrees for 20 -25 minutes.

Recipe _____

Ingredients:

Method:

Recipe

Ingredients:

Method:

Recipe _____

Ingredients:

Method:

Fire for men, is the fairest gift,
and power to see the sun;
health as well, if a man may have it,
and a life not stained with sin.

Campfire cooking

Eating outside, enjoying the weather-campfire cooking should be a straightforward, one-pot deal. A Blot at home wouldn't feel complete without getting the fire-pit going, and a good celebration deserves better than pink-in-the-middle sausages or boring baked potatoes.

<u>Beany Chilli</u>

Warm yourself by the campfire with this vegetarian chilli. Serve with cheesy nacho chips.

Serves 4

Ingredients:

- Olive oil
- 2 onions (chopped)
- 2 garlic cloves (grated)
- ½ tsp chilli flakes
- 1 tsp cinnamon
- 1 tsp ground cumin
- 1 tsp cayenne pepper
- 1 tsp smoked paprika
- 1 tsp dried oregano
- 2 courgettes (chopped into smallish pieces)
- 2 red peppers (chopped into smallish pieces)
- 1 tin of chopped tomatoes
- 1 tin of kidney beans
- 1 tin of borlotti beans
- 187ml red bottle (a tiny wine bottle)
- Handful of chopped coriander
- Salt & pepper (to taste)

Method:

Heat some oil in a large pan, add the onions and fry for several minutes, to soften.

Add the rest of the ingredients to the pan and simmer for about 30 minutes, stirring occasionally.

Fennel, Courgette & Chicken Kebabs

This works best in the summer with fresh veg, and served with a glass of last year's parsnip wine.

Serve with rice.

Serves 2

Ingredients:

- 2 chicken breasts (cut into chunks)
- 1 courgette (sliced & quartered)
- ½ a fennel bulb (cut into cubes)
- 1 tsp fennel seeds
- Juice of 1 lemon
- Salt & pepper

Method:

Put the lemon juice and fennel seeds into a bowl and season with salt & pepper.

Add the chunks of chicken and mix well. Leave to marinade for about an hour.

Place the chicken, fennel and courgette, in turn, onto 4 skewers.

Cook over a barbeque or fire for 5 - 10 minutes, turning occasionally, until cooked through.

Lamb Rogan Josh

What can be better than eating a curry with a glass of home brewed beer, sitting by the fire with friends?

Serve with flatbreads

Serves 4

Ingredients:

- Groundnut oil
- 1 onion (peeled and finely chopped)
- 1 fresh chilli (finely chopped)
- Thumb sized piece of ginger (peeled and grated)
- 800g lamb neck (cut into 2cm chunks)
- small bunch of coriander (finely chopped)
- 4 bay leaves
- 1 tin of chopped tomatoes
- 1 red pepper (chopped)
- 150g Rogan josh paste
- 800ml of water
- 2 handfuls of red lentils
- Salt & pepper (to taste)
- Handful of spinach

Method:

Heat some oil in a large pan and add the onion, chilli and ginger.

Cook for a few minutes.

Add the rest of the ingredients, apart from the spinach and cook for about an hour.

Remove the bay leaves and add the spinach. Mix well and serve.

Spicy Tomato Pasta

This versatile recipe can use any vegetables you have a glut of-add courgettes, runner beans, or fresh chillies as they become available.

serves 2

Ingredients:

- 300g Pasta
- 1 tin chopped tomatoes
- 10 Cherry tomatoes (halved)
- 1 courgette (sliced and quartered)
- 1 red pepper (deseeded and chopped)
- 1 pinch of chilli flakes
- Salt & pepper

Method:

Cook the pasta, following the packet instructions.

Drain the pasta and add the rest of the ingredients. Return to the heat and cook on a low heat for a few minutes, stirring occasionally until warm through.

<u>Chilli, Ginger & Lime Mackerel Fillets</u>

Mackerel is a good oily fish that can hold its own against this spicy marinade.

Serve with flatbreads or rice

Serves 2

Ingredients:

- Olive oil
- 4 Mackerel fillets
- ½ teaspoon of ground ginger
- juice of 1 lime
- ½ a teaspoon of chilli flakes
- salt & pepper

Method:

Put the Ginger, lime and chilli into a bowl and season with salt and pepper.

Add some oil to a frying pan and place the mackerel skin side down in the pan.

Brush the ginger/chilli mix over the fillets.

Cook for a few minutes on both sides, till cooked through.

Chocolate Banana Melt

We're not sure if a banana still counts as one of your five a day after you've wrapped it in marshmallow and chocolate, but once in a while can't do any harm.

Ingredients:

- 1 banana
- 2 tablespoons mini marshmallows
- 2 tablespoons chocolate chips

Method:

Slice the banana in half, lengthways, and place onto some foil.

Fill the sliced banana with chocolate chips and marshmallows.

Wrap the foil tightly around the banana and cook on a grill over the campfire for a few minutes.

Damper on a Stick

This popular New Zealand recipe was provided by Chris Butcher who says to eat them with golden syrup.

Makes 2

Ingredients:

- 1 cup self-raising flour
- 1 tsp sugar
- 1 tbsp. butter
- 1 cup milk
- pinch of salt

Method:

Rub the butter through the flour until it is all crumbly.

Mix the salt, sugar and milk in until it forms a dough.

Divide into two pieces and roll into a snake shape. Wind around a clean skewer.

Hold over the campfire to cook.

Recipe _____

Ingredients:

Method:

Recipe _____

Ingredients:

Method:

Recipe _____

Ingredients:

Method:

He must early go forth whose workers are few,
himself his work to seek;
much remains undone for the morning-sleeper,
for the swift is wealth half won.

Breakfasts

Breakfast is probably the meal we think least about, often relying on routine or convenience. Here are a few simple ideas to help you feel more creative in the mornings.

Raspberry and Honey Pancakes

With pancake day approaching we needed to come up with an egg and milk free pancake.

The almond milk gives a great flavour to the pancakes, but Soya or any other milk would also work.

I like to make mini pancakes using crumpet rings as they are a bit easier to handle.

Ingredients:

300ml almond milk

100g self-raising flour (sieved)

Pinch of salt

Dairy free spread, like Flora

3 tablespoons of juice from a can of chickpeas (lightly beaten)

To serve:

Honey

Raspberries

Method:

Add half the milk to the flour and salt and whisk to a smooth mix. Add the rest of the milk and the chickpea juice and whisk again.

Place a couple of crumpet rings into a small frying pan. Add a small amount of spread to each ring. Pour some batter into the rings and cook on a low heat for several minutes.

Carefully remove the rings and flip the pancakes. Cook for a few more minutes, until golden in colour.

Serve drizzled in honey and with a handful of raspberries.

Spicy Scrambled Eggs

Spicy food is the perfect way to wake yourself up in the morning. The capsicum in chilli is a stimulant that can be addictive and actually makes people happy!

Serves 2

Ingredients:

4 eggs (lightly whisked)

12 cherry tomatoes (halved)

2 spring onions (finely chopped)

Pinch of hot chilli flakes

1 teaspoon cumin seeds

Splash of milk

Salt & pepper

Method:

Stick all the ingredients into a pan and cook on a low heat for several minutes, stirring occasionally, until cooked through.

Serve on crusty toasted bread.

Mush

I got the original version of this recipe from Chris Butcher, who says it's the perfect hangover cure.

Here's my take on it.

Serves 2

Ingredients:

500g potatoes (peeled and chopped up small)

8 rashers of bacon (cut into pieces)

10 cherry tomatoes (halved)

4 eggs

Olive oil

A pinch of chilli flakes (optional)

Salt & pepper

Cheese (grated)

Method:

Boil the potatoes for 10 minutes and drain.

Add the bacon to the pan and drizzle with olive oil. Cook for a few minutes, until the potatoes and bacon start to crisp.

Add the tomatoes and the eggs and mix well. Cook for several minutes.

Season with salt and pepper, add the chilli flakes, if using and stir through.

Serve topped with grated cheese

Garlic Mushrooms

Quick, simple, and healthy - serve as a topping on a couple of slices of sourdough toast if you need something more filling.

Serves 2

Ingredients:

4 large Portobello mushrooms

2 cloves of garlic (grated)

½ teaspoon of rosemary (finely chopped)

½ teaspoon of thyme (finely chopped)

Tablespoon of olive oil

Salt & pepper (to taste)

Method:

Heat some oil in a pan and add the mushrooms, bottoms up. Brush the tops of the mushrooms with a little oil.

Cook on a medium heat for 2 to 3 minutes.

Turn the mushrooms bottom down and add the herbs to the tops. Season with salt and pepper.

Stick the garlic into the pan. Cook for several minutes whilst moving the mushrooms around the pan.

Kedgeree

A traditional, spicy breakfast that takes as long as a fry-up but with a lot less fat.

Serves 4

Ingredients:

4 eggs (boiled and quartered)

300g skinless smoked haddock

1 bay leaf

150g basmati rice

Olive oil

1 thumb-sized piece fresh ginger (peeled and grated)

1 medium onion (finely chopped)

1 fresh red chilli (finely chopped)

1 clove garlic (grated)

1 tablespoons curry powder

1 tablespoon mustard seeds

10 Cherry tomatoes (halved)

Juice of a lemon

A handful of fresh coriander (finely chopped)

Salt & Pepper

Method:

Put the fish and bay leaf into a pan and cover with water. Bring to the boil and simmer for about 5 minutes, until cooked through. Remove the fish from the pan and leave to cool. Break into chunks with a fork.

Cook and drain the rice. Set aside.

Heat some olive oil in a frying pan. Add the ginger, onion, chilli and garlic and cook on a low heat for about 5 minutes. Add the curry powder and mustard seeds and cook for a few minutes.

Add the tomatoes, lemon juice, fish and rice to the pan and gently heat through. Add the eggs and the coriander, season with salt & pepper and stir through.

Recipe

Ingredients:

Method:

Recipe

Ingredients:

Method:

Recipe _____

Ingredients:

Method:

No great thing needs, a man to give,
oft little will purchase praise;
with half a loaf and a half-filled cup
A friend full fast I made

Bread

Humans have been baking for a long time. The origins of bread appear to go back to the Egyptians. Early breads would have been flat, fried over hot stones or in the ashes of the hearth.

Originally a part of the process for making beer, we eventually started baking using sourdoughs and the dregs from brewing. You can still make bread using this Method now and I have even made breads using beer, instead of water, to give a lovely malty flavour to the bread.

There is nothing like the smell of fresh bread. I haven't really been baking for very long and so I'm by no means an expert, however I have become a bit obsessed with perfecting and simplifying my main recipes.

Most experts seem to over complicate things. Bread doesn't need to be complex. A basic loaf only requires flour, yeast, salt and water, about 10 minutes of actual work from you and that's it! By following some simple rules, you can soon be baking your own bread too.

These recipes get progressively harder, but follow the same basic principles all the way through. As with most things, use the best ingredients you can afford; Your baking will benefit from using good quality flour.

Sourdough Starter

A sourdough starter is a simple way of making bread without using shop bought yeast, relying instead on naturally occurring yeasts. This is great for making Rye bread and Sourdough. It gives an amazing flavour to the bread.

It's easy to make your own starter, using naturally occurring yeast from the air in your Kitchen. You will need a large container. I use a container designed for holding a bag of flour, but have also used large Kilner jars. It will need to be about 4 times the size of the original mix to allow for frothing and extra ingredients.

Ingredients:

- Wholemeal bread flour (any kind should work, I like to use rye)
- Water

Method:

Put 150g of flour into a container and add 150ml of warm water and whisk well. It should look a bit like porridge.

After a day or 2 you should start to see signs of fermentation, tiny bubbles. If you smell it, it should be taking on a sharp, fruity, vinegary smell.

Remember that your starter is now a living thing, so it needs feeding and watering regularly, I do it every couple of days.

At this point you can stop measuring amounts and just add a small amount of flour and water and whisk. Keep it to the same porridge like consistency.

Wait a week to 10 days for the starter to establish properly before trying to bake with it.

If liquid forms on the top of your starter at any point, remove this before feeding. The liquid is alcohol and is a sign that your starter is hungry and you are not feeding it regularly enough.

You can remove some of your starter, as you wish, which makes a great opportunity to bake some bread with it!

If you are unable to feed your starter for a period of time, stick it in the fridge. It should keep without being fed for about a week.

Chocolate Rye Bread

Rye flour grows in colder climates. It makes quite dense bread, due to a lack of gluten. This makes kneading it a waste of time, as you can't stretch out the proteins. In Denmark, Rye bread is really popular and bakeries make different kinds including a version of this chocolate rye.

Making this bread is more like making a cake than a bread, so it's a great beginners loaf and will give you the confidence you need to move on to making other breads.

You can also use this recipe to make a normal rye bread by leaving out the chocolate and dates.

Makes a 2lb loaf

Ingredients:

- 300g rye flour
- 100g white bread flour (sifted)
- 100g sourdough starter
- 10g salt
- 1 Teaspoon of olive oil + a little extra
- 300ml warm water (give or take)
- 120g dates
- 50g pumpkin seeds
- 50g linseeds
- 100g dark chocolate (chopped)

Method:

Put the flour and salt into a large bowl and mix together.

Add the starter and the olive oil and slowly add the water and mix together to form quite a sticky dough that is more like a cake mix than a bread dough. You can add more or less water depending on how your dough feels. I find it varies slightly every time.

Add the seeds, dates and chocolate and mix well

Place the dough in a lightly greased loaf tin. Cover loosely with a plastic bag and leave for a few hours, ideally overnight. It won't rise very much due to the low gluten of the rye flour.

Heat your oven to its highest temperature and boil the kettle. Place some water in a baking tray at the bottom of the oven, this will help to create a good crust on your loaf.

Put your loaf in the centre of the oven for 10 minutes before dropping the temperature to 200 degrees if the crust is looking pale, 180 degrees if the crust is noticeably browning, and 170 if it seems to be browning quickly.

Cook for a further 40 mins. I like to take it out of the tin for the last 10 minutes, but this is optional and you may find it is stuck in the tin.

Remove from the tin. The loaf should sound hollow when you tap it on the bottom.

Leave to cool fully before cutting.

Rosemary Sourdough

Sourdough tastes great, but is expensive to buy. It's relatively easy to make and doesn't take up much time, but does need extra time to prove.

It requires the starter recipe from the beginning of this chapter, which takes about a week to establish, but once going is ready to use any time.

You could also use this recipe to make a normal sourdough bread by leaving out the rosemary.

This fills a 2 lb loaf tin, or 500g proving basket

Ingredients:

- 500g white bread flour (sifted)
- 10g salt
- 160g sourdough starter
- 25g honey
- 1 teaspoon of olive oil + a little extra
- 300ml warm water (give or take)
- 2 teaspoons chopped rosemary
- A small amount of rye flour for coating

Method:

Put the flour and salt into a large bowl and mix together.

Add the starter, honey, rosemary and olive oil and slowly add the water and mix together to form a slightly sticky dough. It needs to be workable, but a slightly wetter dough will make a better loaf. You can add more or less water depending on how your dough feels. I find it varies slightly every time.

Tip it out onto your worktop and knead for 10 minutes. I don't bother to flour or oil the worktop, I never really found it necessary.

There are various ways to knead your dough. I like to stretch it out, then roll it back in and give it a 90 degree turn, before stretching it out again. Check out 'The Homegrown Forager' on Youtube or Facebook for a video of this technique.

Put your dough into a lightly oiled bowl and cover loosely with a plastic bag to stop it drying out. Place somewhere warm, I usually put it near our wood-burner or in the conservatory on a warm day.

Leave to prove for several hours until the dough has roughly doubled in size. Sourdough takes longer to develop than bread made with shop bought yeast, but benefits from the extra time, as it develops a better flavour.

Tip your dough back out onto your work surface and carefully deflate it by poking it with your fingers. Reshape and coat with rye flour.

Place it in a lightly greased loaf tin for a square sandwich loaf, or into a heavily floured proving basket, if you have one, for a more traditional loaf. Cover loosely with a plastic bag and leave for another hour or more to prove again. If using a tin, it should rise to the top.

Heat your oven to its highest temperature and boil the kettle. If using the proving basket option also place an oven tray in too heat.

Place some water in a baking tray at the bottom of the oven, this will help to create a good crust on your loaf.

If using the proving basket, tip your bread out onto the hot oven tray and get it in the oven and shut the door, as quick as possible, to avoid heat loss. If using a loaf tin, put your loaf tin in the centre of the oven.

Cook for 10 minutes before dropping the temperature to 200 degrees if the crust is looking pale, 180 degrees if the crust is noticeably browning, and 170 if it seems to be browning quickly. Cook for a further 40 mins.

When using a loaf tin, I like to take it out of the tin for the last 10 minutes.

Remove from the oven, the loaf should sound hollow when you tap it on the bottom.

Leave to cool fully before cutting.

Black bread

We first tried black bread at Midgardsblot festival in Norway. It's an interesting flavour. Originally found in an early Viking age grave in Sweden, it was baked using yeast from the same family as brewing today, pointing to brewing waste being used to rise the bread.

This version is made following a basic sourdough recipe, but cooked using blood.

This fills a 2 lb loaf tin, or 500g proving basket

Ingredients:

- 250g white bread flour (sifted)
- 250g wholemeal flour
- 10g salt
- 160g sourdough starter
- 1 Teaspoon of olive oil
- 300ml warm water (give or take)
- 40 ml dried blood
- A small amount of rye flour for coating

Method:

Mix the dried blood with the water and whisk to a smooth consistency.

Put the flour and salt into a large bowl and mix together.

Add the starter and olive oil and slowly add the blood solution and mix together to form a slightly sticky dough. It needs to be workable, but a slightly wetter dough will make a better loaf. You can add more or less water depending on how your dough feels. I find it varies slightly every time.

Tip out onto your worktop and knead for 10 minutes. I don't bother to flour or oil the worktop, I never really found it necessary.

There are various ways to knead your dough. I like to stretch it out, then roll it back in and give it a 90 degree turn, before stretching it out again. Check out 'The Homegrown forager' on Youtube or Facebook for a video of this technique.

Put your dough into a lightly oiled bowl and cover loosely with a plastic bag to stop it drying out. Place somewhere warm, I usually put it near our wood-burner or in the conservatory on a warm day.

Leave to prove for several hours until the dough has roughly doubled in size. Sourdough takes longer to develop than bread made with shop bought yeast, but benefits from the extra time, as it develops a better flavour.

Tip your dough back out onto your work surface and carefully deflate it by poking it with your fingers. Reshape and coat with rye flour.

Place it in a lightly greased loaf tin for a square sandwich loaf, or into a heavily floured proving basket, if you have one, for a more traditional loaf. Cover loosely with a plastic bag and leave for another hour or more to prove again. If using a tin, it should rise to the top.

Heat your oven to its highest temperature and boil the kettle. If using the proving basket option also place an oven tray in too heat.

Place some water in a baking tray at the bottom of the oven, this will help to create a good crust on your loaf.

If using the proving basket, tip your bread out onto the hot oven tray and get it in the oven and shut the door, as quick as possible, to avoid heat loss. If using a loaf tin, put your loaf tin in the centre of the oven.

Cook for 10 minutes before dropping the temperature to 200 degrees if the crust is looking pale, 180 degrees if the crust is noticeably browning, and 170 if it seems to be browning quickly. Cook for a further 40 mins.

When using a loaf tin, I like to take it out of the tin for the last 10 minutes.

Remove from the oven, the loaf should sound hollow when you tap it on the bottom.

Leave to cool fully before cutting.

Garlic Sourdough Flatbreads

Early breads would probably have been fried flatbreads, just like this recipe. Flavours like Garlic and rosemary were very popular, so there is every possibility that a bread like this one could have been made.

Makes 4 small flatbreads

Ingredients:

- 200g white bread flour (sifted) + a little extra
- 5g salt
- 100g sourdough starter
- Tablespoon of olive oil + a little extra for frying
- 180 ml warm water (give or take)
- 1 or 2 garlic cloves, grated (to taste)

Method:

Put the flour and salt into a large bowl and mix together.

Add the starter, garlic and olive oil; and slowly add the water and mix together to form a dough. It needs to be workable, but a slightly wetter dough will make a better bread. You can add more or less water depending on how your dough feels. I find it varies slightly every time.

Tip out onto your worktop and knead for 5 minutes. I don't bother to flour or oil the worktop, I never really found it necessary.

There are various ways to knead your dough I like to stretch it out, then roll it back in and give it a 90 degree turn, before stretching it out again. Check out 'The Homegrown Forager' on YouTube or Facebook for a video of this technique.

Put your dough into a lightly oiled bowl and cover loosely with a plastic bag to stop it drying out. Place somewhere warm, I usually put it near our wood-burner or in the conservatory on a warm day.

Leave to prove for several hours until the dough has roughly doubled in size. Sourdough takes longer to develop than bread made with shop bought yeast, but benefits from the extra time, as it develops a better flavour.

Flour your work surface and break your dough into 4 portions. Cover each portion with a coat of flour and squash to around 3 or 4 mm thick.

Heat some olive oil in a frying pan and cook each flatbread for 3 or 4 minutes on each side.

Garlic Baguettes

This recipe started off as an experiment and due to an error, turned out really good, and now I always make it this way. The error is the large amount of yeast. This creates big holes in the baguettes, a lot like in a sourdough.

Makes 2 small baguettes

Ingredients:

- 500g white bread flour (sifted)
- 10g salt
- 20g dried bread yeast
- 300ml warm water (give or take)
- 4 garlic cloves (grated)

Method:

Put the flour and salt into a large bowl and mix together.

Add the yeast and garlic, then slowly add the water and mix together to form a dough. You can add more or less water depending on how your dough feels. I find it varies slightly every time.

Tip out onto your worktop and knead for 10 minutes. I don't bother to flour or oil the worktop, I never really found it necessary.

There are various ways to knead your dough I like to stretch it out, then roll it back in and give it a 90 degree turn, before stretching it out again. Check out 'The Homegrown forager' on Youtube or Facebook for a video of this technique.

Put your dough into a lightly oiled bowl and cover loosely with a plastic bag to stop it drying out. Place somewhere warm, I usually put it near our wood-burner or in the conservatory on a warm day.

Leave to prove for about 2 hours until the dough has roughly doubled in size.

Tip your dough back out onto your work surface and carefully deflate it by poking it with your fingers. Divide the dough into 2 and shape into baguettes.

Place the baguettes into a lightly greased baguette baking tray.

Heat your oven to its highest temperature and boil the kettle.

Place some water in a baking tray at the bottom of the oven, this will help to create a good crust on your baguettes.

Add a little olive oil to the tops of the baguettes and slash the tops with a sharp, serrated knife. Put your baguette tray in the centre of the oven.

Cook for 10 minutes before dropping the temperature to 200 degrees if the crust is looking pale, 180 degrees if the crust is noticeably browning, and 170 if it seems to be browning quickly. Cook for a further 30 mins.

Remove from the oven and serve whilst still warm.

Everyday Loaf

This recipe is really simple. The bread is the perfect size for sandwiches and toast. I make it in batches at the weekend and freeze it as half-loaves for use during the week.

This fills a 4 lb loaf tin

Ingredients:

- 500g wholemeal flour
- 500g white bread flour (sifted)
- 20g salt
- 10g bread yeast
- 2 handfuls of sunflower seeds (optional)
- Tablespoon of olive oil + a little extra
- 700ml warm water (give or take)

Method:

Put all of the dry ingredients into a large bowl. Make sure you keep the salt separate from the yeast, otherwise you will kill your yeast. Carefully mix the dry ingredients together.

Add the olive oil and slowly add the water and mix together to form a dough. The dough should be quite sticky, but still workable without getting it stuck to your hands. Add more or less water depending on how your dough feels. I find it varies slightly every time.

Tip out onto your worktop and knead for 10 minutes. I don't bother to flour or oil the worktop, as it's not really necessary.

There are various ways to knead your dough I like to stretch it out, then roll it back in and give it a 90 degree turn, before stretching it out again. Check out 'The Homegrown forager' on Youtube or Facebook for a video of this technique.

Put your dough into a lightly oiled bowl and cover loosely with a plastic bag to stop it drying out. Place somewhere warm, I usually put it near our wood-burner or in the conservatory on a warm day. Leave to prove for an hour or two until the dough has roughly doubled in size.

Tip your dough back out onto your work surface and carefully deflate it by poking it with your fingers. Reshape and place it in a lightly greased loaf tin. Cover loosely with a plastic bag and leave for another hour or more to prove again. Its ready to bake when the loaf has expanded and filled the tin.

Heat your oven to its highest temperature and boil the kettle. Place some water in a baking tray at the bottom of the oven, this will help to create a good crust on your loaf.

Put your loaf in the centre of the oven for 10 minutes before dropping the temperature to 200 degrees if the crust is looking pale, 180 degrees if the crust is noticeably browning, and 170 if it seems to be browning quickly. Cook for a further 50 mins.

Remove from the tin and leave to cool fully before cutting.

Recipe _____

Ingredients:

Method:

Recipe _____

Ingredients:

Method:

Recipe

Ingredients:

Method:

Recipe _____

Ingredients:

Method:

He welcomes the night, whose fare is enough,
Short are the yards of a ship,
uneasy are autumn nights;
full oft does the weather, change in a week,
and more in a month's time.

Jams & Preserves

Preserving gluts of produce and foraged goods has been an essential part of human life for most of history.

Depending on the time and location, preserving Methods included drying and salting, as well as pickling in vinegar and alcohol, and preserving in sugar.

Today it has largely fallen out of practice for many people, probably due to how spoilt we are for choice of unseasonal goods in the shops.

Those that do preserve mainly do so for the flavour, or because they grew too many courgettes in the garden and don't know what to do with them!

Personally, we like cooking stews in the winter with pickled greens and beets, and there's nothing better than spreading a layer of crab apple jelly on toast to remind us of those oh so rare sunny summer days.

Make sure to sterilise all storage containers and jars before filling. Give them a wash with warm soapy water and place in the oven at 100 degrees for about 10 minutes. Pot the jams and preserves whilst the jars are still warm.

When making jams, stick a saucer in the freezer when you begin. Then, when you think your jam is ready, put a small amount on to the saucer and after a minute or so, push the jam with your finger. If it crinkles, as if it has a skin forming, then it is ready to put into your jars. Check out 'The Homegrown Forager' on Facebook or Youtube for a video example of this.

Lemon Curd

Homemade lemon curd tastes great and is a good way to use up a glut of eggs. It's easy to make and should keep for around a month, if you can make it last that long!

Ingredients:

- 7 Eggs
- 8 lemons (rind and juice)
- 200g Butter
- 400g caster sugar

Method:

Melt the butter in a pan. Whilst you wait beat the eggs.

Once the butter has melted add the rest of the ingredients to the pan and whisk together.

Don't worry if the mixture looks like it's curdling, it should eventually come together. Give it a mix/beat every few minutes.

Heat for around 10 mins until thick and creamy, but avoid boiling.

Carefully pour into warm sterilised jars and seal. Store in a cool dry place and refrigerate once opened.

Fiery Ginger Marmalade

This is unusual, but a great way to use up the summer glut of courgettes and marrows that every grower tends to end up struggling with at some point.

Ingredients:

- 4 lemons (zest and juice)
- 1kg courgette or marrow, peeled and grated on the large holes of a grater
- 1kg jam sugar
- 100g peeled and grated root ginger
- 200g crystallised stem ginger

Method:

Put the lemon juice, zest and courgette into a large pan and warm gently to release some of the juices.

Add the sugar and the ginger and bring to the boil. Simmer for around 10 - 15 minutes until setting point is reached.

Leave to cool for 10 minutes, before pouring into warm, sterilised jars.

Crab Apple Jelly

I love stocking the cupboard with crab apple jelly, it's great spread on toast or served with pork. It's a fantastic pinky orange colour.

It amazes me that no one else seems to pick the small, scabby looking apples, which you can find everywhere. It doesn't take long to fill a bag. I usually come home with several bags full late in September.

High in pectin, there is no need to use jam sugar with these apples. Try adding other wild fruits, such as blackberries, to the mix.

Ingredients:

- 1kg crab apples
- Up to 1kg granulated sugar
- Water

Method:

Put the fruit into a large pan and cover with water. Simmer until the fruit starts to fall apart.

Strain through a muslin. Leave to drip for several hours or overnight, but whatever you do avoid squeezing or you'll end up with cloudy jelly.

Measure the liquid and for every 600ml of juice, you'll need 450 kg of sugar. Put the juice into a pan and bring to the boil.

Add the sugar and stir until dissolved.

Slowly bring to a rolling boil and boil rapidly, without stirring, for about 10 minutes until setting point is reached.

Pour into warm, sterilised jars.

Blackberry Jam

I rarely see anyone out picking blackberries anymore, yet in the shops they sell for over £2 for not much more than a handful!

Any land even slightly overgrown seems to have at least a few blackberries growing on it.

They are incredibly versatile. We use them for jams and wines, as well as in whisky, and in crumbles.

Ingredients:

- 1kg blackberries
- 1kg jam sugar
- Juice of 2 lemons

Method:

Heat the fruit in a large pan with the lemon juice, add the sugar and stir until dissolved.

Slowly bring to a rolling boil and boil rapidly, without stirring, for about 10 - 15 minutes until setting point is reached.

Pour into warm, sterilised jars.

Damson Jelly

This was one of my granddad's favourite jams and is a lovely pinky purple colour.

The damson is the wild cousin of the plum, and also related to bullaces and sloes. It's slightly smaller than a plum and a little on the sour side.

I only know of one location locally to me where they grow, but if you can find a tree, it's well worth picking them, for this jelly, or as an alternative to sloes in sloe gin.

Ingredients:

- 1 kg damsons (or plums)
- Up to 1kg granulated sugar
- Water

Method:

Put the fruit into a large pan and half cover with water. Simmer until the fruit starts to fall apart.

Strain through a muslin. Leave to drip for several hours or overnight, but whatever you do avoid squeezing or you'll end up with cloudy jelly.

Measure the liquid and for every 600ml of juice, you'll need 450 kg of sugar. Put the juice into a pan and bring to the boil.

Add the sugar and stir until dissolved.

Slowly bring to a rolling boil and boil rapidly, without stirring, for about 10 minutes until setting point is reached.

Pour into warm, sterilised jars.

Rhubarb & Vanilla Jam

The vanilla in this jam compliments the sharpness of the rhubarb. Whilst you can't eat the leaves, they do have other uses; They can be used to make natural pesticides or to add colour to fabrics. Interestingly the plant also contains the same chemical used to make bleach.

Ingredients:

- 1kg rhubarb (cut into 2 cm pieces, leaves removed)
- 1kg jam sugar
- Juice of 2 lemons
- 2 vanilla pods (halved)

Method:

Gently heat the rhubarb in a large pan with the lemon juice and vanilla pod for a few minutes

Add the sugar and stir until dissolved.

Slowly bring to a rolling boil and boil rapidly, without stirring, for about 10 - 15 minutes until setting point is reached.

Leave to cool for 10 minutes, remove the vanilla pods and pour into warm, sterilised jars.

<u>Sweet Chilli Jam</u>

This spicy jam is perfect with meats and cheeses or for dipping prawns into. I usually make a lot of it in the summer using Homegrown chillies.

You can easily vary the heat by changing the type of chilli you use to match your own taste.

Ingredients:

- 840g sweet red peppers (deseeded and top removed)
- 100g chillies (tops removed)
- 2 cloves garlic (peeled)
- 50g ginger
- 1kg jam sugar
- Juice of 4 limes
- 200ml cider vinegar
- ½ tsp salt

Method:

Blitz the peppers, chillies, ginger and garlic in a food processor to a fine pulp.

Add all the ingredients to a large pan and heat gently whilst stirring to dissolve the sugar.

Slowly bring to a rolling boil and boil rapidly, without stirring, for about 10 minutes until setting point is reached.

Leave to cool for 10 minutes before pouring into warm, sterilised jars.

Chutney

This recipe is great for using up the end of season tomatoes that didn't have time to ripen before autumn, combined with the last of the summer glut of courgettes, and freshly foraged crab apples.

Ingredients:

- 1kg courgettes (diced)
- 1kg green tomatoes (diced)
- 500g crab apples (cored and diced)
- 500g shallots (peeled and diced)
- 500g sultanas
- 500g Muscovado sugar
- 600ml cider vinegar
- 1 chilli (finely chopped)
- Pinch of salt
- For the spice bag:
- 50g fresh ginger
- 2 garlic cloves (peeled)
- 12 cloves
- 2 teaspoons black peppercorns
- 1 teaspoon black mustard seeds

Method:

Tie the spice bag ingredients into a piece of muslin and put it into a large pan. Add the rest of the ingredients and bring to the boil.

Simmer for 2 ½ – 3 hours until reduced and thick. It's ready if you can draw a spoon through it to reveal the base of the pan for a few seconds.

Spoon into warm, sterile jars and mature for a few months before eating.

This will keep for a couple of years.

Mulled Pears

Sweet and Christmassy, a jar of this would make a good gift for any foodie friends.

Ingredients:

- 1.5kg Pears (peeled, halved and cored)
- 150g granulated sugar
- 500ml dry Cider
- cloves
- 2 cinnamon sticks
- 2 star anise

Method:

Pre-heat the oven to 150 degrees.

Heat the cider in a pan with the sugar, until it's dissolved.

Stud the pears with a few cloves and put them into a large Kilner jar with the cinnamon sticks and star anise.

Pour over the cider and place in the oven for 1 hour, without the lid on.

Remove from the oven and put the lid on.

Leave to cool. This will keep for up to 1 year.

Pickled Beets

We like to eat this in winter stews or in the summer with cured meats and cheeses.

Ingredients:

- 1kg beetroot (sliced)
- 1 tbsp. black peppercorns
- 2 teaspoons of salt
- 1 tbsp. coriander seeds
- 1 tbsp. yellow mustard seeds
- 10 cloves
- pinch of dried chilli flakes (optional)
- 700ml cider vinegar, plus 3½ tbsp.
- 100g light brown soft sugar

Method:

Pack the beetroot into warm, sterile jars.

Stick the rest of the ingredients in to a pan and bring to a boil. Simmer for a few minutes.

Pour the hot vinegar over the beetroot and seal immediately. Ready to eat in a couple of weeks but will keep for at least 2 years.

Recipe

Ingredients:

Method:

Recipe

Ingredients:

Method:

Recipe _____

Ingredients:

Method:

Recipe

Ingredients:

Method:

Shun not the mead, but drink in measure;
speak to the point or be still;
for rudeness none, shall rightly blame thee
if soon thy bed thou seekest.

Alcoholic Drinks

Mead has a unique status in heathenry. In the myth of its creation, it has divine origins; the gods make wise Kvasir from their spit, and his blood is brewed into mead, which Odin steals from the giants - the few drops he loses on his flight home become a source of inspiration for the artists and poets of Midgard.

Throughout history, mead and other wines were too expensive for most people, and for some, drinking it with guests at special occasions may have been a sacrifice in itself.

Despite the modern heathens love of mead, beer was much more common, and a weak beer would have been brewed for everyday drinking.

First Steps

I love making my own booze, it's great fun and the results taste fantastic. There are a few basic rules that you need to follow. I won't go into detail here, as there are plenty of books out there that do it better, and I really want this to be as simple as possible so that brewing doesn't seem daunting.

The first rule of making any kind of brew, is to make sure you sterilise everything. Buckets, bottles, syphons - everything that comes into contact with your brew. You can buy sterilising powder in home-brew shops, Wilko's or online. Follow the directions on the packet and clean everything thoroughly. Once clean, rinse the equipment well.

The next thing is to make sure you have a hydrometer. These are cheap to buy and will help you to know when your brew is finished fermenting. It will also enable you to estimate the alcohol content of your finished brew.

- Take a reading before you add your yeast. This is known as the Original gravity or OG
- Take another at the end. This is known as the Final gravity or FG
- Using a simple formula, (OG - FG) x 0.13 = %, you can then figure out the alcohol content of your finished brew
- For example, if your original gravity is 1080 and your final gravity is 1000, then using the formula (1080 - 1000) x 0.13 = 10.4% alcohol content

The original gravity of most wines and meads should start at around 1050 - 1100

The original gravity for beer should start at around 1040

The higher the number, the higher the potential alcohol content of your brew, however this is also limited by the type of yeast used.

Your brew will either finish fermenting when the yeast runs out of food (sugar) or when the alcohol content is too high for the yeast to live in.

When your brew stops bubbling, or slows to less than 1 bubble a minute, use the hydrometer to see if your brew is finished fermenting. Move your brew somewhere warm and check the gravity over a period of 3 days and if the reading doesn't change, fermentation has stopped.

At this stage, there are a few optional things you can add to your brew. Not everyone does, but I like too.

122

The first 2 things are fermentation stopper, and campden tablets. These are generally added at the same time to wine, mead and cider, and help to stabilise the alcohol by killing off any yeast that might still be hanging around. They also help to prevent any bacterial growth during the ageing process. Add these as per the packet instructions, usually you'll need to stir your brew daily for 3 days after adding, which will also help to remove any trapped co2.

The next thing is bentonite. This is a naturally occurring clay that draws particles from the alcohol and settles it to the bottom of your container. This clears the alcohol, so you can syphon your liquid into a new container or bottle to prevent a hazy wine.

Mead

Today mead is enjoyed and used as offerings so often in heathenry that, though not necessary, a celebration doesn't feel complete without it.

Ingredients:

- Clear honey - 2kg for sweet/1.7kg/for medium/1.4kg for dry
- 4.5 l water
- 2 teaspoons of citric acid (or the juice and rind of 2 lemons)
- 1 teaspoon of wine yeast (I use Young's super wine yeast compound
- 1 campden tablet (optional)
- 1 teaspoon fermentation stopper (optional)
- 1 teaspoon Bentonite (optional)

Method:

Put the honey into the bucket with 2 litres of boiled water and stir until dissolved.

Add the citric acid and 2.5 litres of cold water.

Make a note of the gravity.

When the liquid has cooled to room temperature, add the yeast. Leave to ferment for 3 days.

Strain the liquid into a 5 litre Demijohn, fit with an airlock and leave to ferment until it stops bubbling-this depends on the general surrounding temperature.

When fermentation ends (bubbles passing through the airlock at less than one a minute) add a crushed campden tablet and fermentation stopper, if using, as per the instructions on the packet.

After 3 days clear the wine by adding bentonite, if using, as per the instructions on the packet.

Don't forget to check your final gravity, if you haven't already, and want to know the percentage of alcohol in your brew.

Finally, syphon the mead into bottles and cork. Age for a minimum of 6 months before drinking.

Parsnip Wine

Finally, a use for parsnips! I can't stand eating them, but this wine is amazing. Well worth the little effort needed and really cheap to make. Watch out though, it's pretty strong stuff.

You could also swap the parsnips for carrots and follow the same recipe.

Ingredients:

- 2 kg parsnips (cut into 5mm pieces)
- 4.5l water
- 1.4 kg granulated sugar
- 2 teaspoons of citric acid (or juice & rind of 2 lemons)
- 1 teaspoon tannin (or a strong cup of black tea)
- 1 teaspoon pectolase (to prevent pectin haze)
- 1 teaspoon of wine yeast (I use Youngs super wine yeast extract)
- 1 campden tablet (optional)
- 1 teaspoon fermentation stopper (optional)
- 1 teaspoon Bentonite (optional)

Method:

Boil 2.5 litres of water and add the parsnips. Boil for around 20 to 25 mins until soft, but not falling apart, otherwise the wine will never clear.

Strain the water from the parsnips into a bucket, add the sugar, citric acid, tannin and pectolase and stir well.

Mix in 2 litres of cold water and finally add your yeast. Check your gravity and make a note of it. Cover loosely for 3 days before straining into a demijohn with an airlock.

When fermentation ends (bubbles passing through the airlock at less than one a minute) add a crushed campden tablet and fermentation stopper, if using, as per the instructions on the packet.

After 3 days clear the wine by adding bentonite, if using, as per the instructions on the packet. Don't forget to check your final gravity, if you haven't already and want to know the percentage of alcohol in your brew.

Finally, syphon the wine into bottles and cork. Age for a minimum of 6 months before drinking.

Ginger Wine

This one is super easy to make and great on a cold winter evening by the fire. I have started to make 5 gallon batches as it never seems to last long enough!

Ingredients:

- 50g root ginger
- 1.5kg granulated sugar
- 100g raisins
- 2 tsp of citric acid (or the juice and rind of 2 lemons)
- 4.5l water (boiled)
- 1 tsp of wine yeast (I use Youngs super wine yeast extract)
- 1 campden tablet (optional)
- 1 teaspoon fermentation stopper (optional)
- 1 teaspoon Bentonite (optional)
- 350ml brandy

Method:

Grate the ginger into a bucket, add the sugar, raisins, citric acid and 2.5l boiled water and stir well.

Mix in 2 litres of cold water and finally add your yeast. Check and make a note of the gravity.

Cover loosely for 1 week before straining into a demijohn with an airlock.

When fermentation ends (bubbles passing through the airlock at less than one a minute) add a crushed campden tablet and fermentation stopper, if using, as per the instructions on the packet.

After 3 days clear the wine by adding bentonite, if using, as per the instructions on the packet.

Don't forget to check your final gravity, if you haven't already and want to know the percentage of alcohol in your brew.

Finally, share the brandy between your bottles, syphon the wine in and cork. Age for a minimum of 6 months before drinking.

Elderberry and Blackberry Wine

This recipe is great heated, but not boiling, with a jar of honey, a few cloves, some grated nutmeg, ¼ pint of water and the juice and rind of a lemon. Add half a small bottle of brandy before serving. Drink whilst still warm.

We drink this every yule when family visit and we always run out!

You can also make this with just elderberries or just blackberries.

Ingredients:

- 800g elderberries
- 800g blackberries
- 4.5l water (boiled)
- 1.5 kg granulated sugar
- 1 tsp pectic enzyme
- 1 tsp of red wine yeast
- 1 tsp yeast nutrient
- 1 campden tablet (optional)
- 1 teaspoon fermentation stopper (optional)
- 1 teaspoon Bentonite (optional)

Method:

Put all the berries into a large bucket and crush with a rolling pin. Add the sugar, pectic enzyme and cover with 4.5l boiled water. Stir well.

Once cool, make a note of your gravity.

Add your yeast and nutrient and cover loosely for 1 week before straining into a demijohn with an airlock.

When fermentation ends (bubbles passing through the airlock at less than one a minute) add a crushed campden tablet and fermentation stopper, if using, as per the instructions on the packet.

After 3 days clear the wine by adding bentonite, if using, as per the instructions on the packet. Don't forget to check your final gravity, if you haven't already and want to know the percentage of alcohol in your brew.

Finally, syphon the wine into bottles and cork.

Age for a minimum of 6 months before drinking, but a year is better.

Elderflower Champagne - make with caution!

This is a low alcohol recipe for a light summer fizz. Every story I know about exploding bottles seems to be connected with this brew. Only store this in plastic soft drink bottles and check regularly that the pressure isn't building up too much, releasing some of the gas if necessary.

This one relies on naturally occurring yeast present in the flowers. Be sure to pick your flowers on a dry day.

Ingredients:

- 800g granulated sugar
- 6L water
- 10 elderflower heads, in full bloom
- 4 lemons

Method:

In a large bucket, dissolve the sugar in 2L boiled water. Once dissolved top up with 4L cold water.

Add the flowers and the juice and rind of the lemons.

Wait for a few days and if your brew hasn't starting to bubble you may need to add a pinch of champagne yeast.

After 6 days of fermenting, strain the liquid through a muslin cloth into sterilised plastic soft drink bottles. Store somewhere safe, that won't cause too much damage, like the shed.

After a week, refrigerate. Open the bottles carefully and serve with ice.

Sloe Gin

September is one of my favourite times of the year, as I get to spend a lot of time outside foraging for fruit. I use this basic recipe for various flavoured liquors. You could also try blackberry whisky, crab apple vodka or rose-hip vodka using the same quantities.

Ingredients:

- 350g Sloes
- 175g granulated Sugar
- 700ml gin

Method:

Wash your fruit and pick out any leaves, twigs, or insects.

Put them into a Kilner jar and cover with the sugar. Pour over the gin and put the lid on.

Shake the jar to mix in the sugar. Shake once a day, for a few days, until the sugar remains dissolved.

After 3 months decant into bottles through a funnel lined with a muslin cloth.

Whilst you can drink this straight away, it does benefit from ageing for a year or more, if you can wait that long.

Idiot Mead

This one comes from Rich Blackett. I met Rich at the first Asgardian festival. He had a bottle of something that I'd overheard was called 'idiot mead'. I was intrigued and he was happy to let me have a taste. It was stronger than expected and it took me by surprise.

Idiot Mead began as an accident. Rich had intended to make some Mead to bring to a Heathen moot. The day before, it was obvious that genuine Mead was not going to be possible.

What he had, was half a bottle of vodka and a few jars of honey.

It's not for everyone, and no substitute for real Mead, but it proved popular enough that he was asked to make it again and now to supply a recipe for this book.

Best enjoyed neat, with a large group of friends.

Ingredients:

- Vodka 35cl
- 1 or 2 jars of honey (to taste)

Method:

Stand the two unopened honey jars in a large pan and fill the pan with hot, not boiling, water. Wait 5 -10mins for the honey to go runny.

Pour a jar of honey into a large Kilner jar and cover with the vodka.

Shake the jar to mix in the vodka. Then shake carefully, until the honey remains dissolved. Taste and add more honey, as required.

Different spirits will complement or contrast with the honey. So, it's worth testing a small amount of honey and any other potential spirits mixers.

I like to use a jar of honey in bourbon whiskey and pop a chilli in it for a few weeks. You could also experiment with adding cinnamon and cloves.

Rosemary and Bay Beer

This one is based on Andy Hamilton's recipe, found in the book 'Booze for free'. It goes down really well and is one of my most popular home brewed beers. Before hops were common in beer brewing, herbs such as rosemary and nettles would have been used, so this is a nice throwback to our ancestors brewing techniques.

If you substitute the rosemary and bay for 35g of dried hops you can also make a simple hop beer.

This beer usually comes out at 4.5 %

Ingredients:

- 5 rosemary sprigs
- 10 bay leaves
- 500g amber malt extract
- 375g sugar
- 12 pints of water
- Beer yeast (or Young's super wine yeast extract)

Method:

Put the rosemary and bay leaves into a large pan and cover with 6 pints of water, boil for 30 minutes.

Meanwhile put your sugar and malt extract into a fermentation bin. Strain the rosemary and bay water through a muslin cloth into the fermentation bin. Stir well to dissolve all the sugar and malt extract.

Pour in 6 pints of cold water and stir. Make a note of the gravity, it should be around 1040.

Add your yeast and leave to ferment for 3 weeks. Whilst a lot of recipes state much shorter times I find the beer benefits from this extended time.

Don't forget to check your final gravity, if you haven't already and want to know the percentage of alcohol in your brew.

Add a level teaspoon of sugar to each beer bottle and syphon the beer into the bottles. Cap the bottles (or use swing tops) and place somewhere warm for 2 days before moving to somewhere cool.

The beer should be ready to drink in 2 weeks, 3 is better.

Pumpkin Beer

Every October I make a big batch of this to see me through the winter. It makes a lovely dark ale, with a slightly sweet tone from the pumpkin.

I have varied the flavour quite significantly by using different types of squash. Butternut works well to give a nutty flavour to the beer.

This beer usually comes out at 4.5 %

Ingredients:

- 1kg pumpkin
- 35g hops
- 500g dark malt extract
- 375g sugar
- 12 pints of water
- Beer yeast (or Young's super wine yeast extract)

Method:

Cut the pumpkin into fist sized pieces and roast for 20 minutes at 200 degrees.

Put the pumpkin into a large pan with the hops and cover with 6 pints of water, boil for 30 minutes.

Meanwhile put your sugar and malt extract into a fermentation bin. Strain the pumpkin water through a muslin cloth into the fermentation bin.

Stir well to dissolve all the sugar and malt extract. Pour in 6 pints of cold water and stir. Make a note of the gravity, it should be around 1040.

Add your yeast and leave to ferment for 3 weeks. Whilst a lot of recipes state much shorter times I find the beer benefits from this extended time.

Don't forget to check your final gravity, if you haven't already and want to know the percentage of alcohol in your brew.

Add a level teaspoon of sugar to each bottle and syphon the beer into the bottles. Cap the bottles (or use swing tops) and place somewhere warm for 2 days before moving to somewhere cool.

The beer should be ready to drink in 2 weeks, 3 is better.

Nettle Beer

A good excuse to get out foraging; nettles are used in place of hops in this recipe, and should be available pretty much everywhere as soon as spring begins.

Try and pick the young leaves from the tops of the plants for a better flavour, and don't pick from plants that have flowered. A thick pair of washing up gloves should be enough to protect you from the stings.

Ingredients:

- 1 carrier bag nearly full of nettle tops
- 500g light malt extract
- 200g sugar
- 175g honey
- 12 pints of water
- 1 teaspoon Young's super wine yeast extract

Method:

Put the nettles into a large pan and cover with 6 pints of water, boil for 30 minutes.

Meanwhile put your sugar, honey and malt extract into a fermentation bin. Strain the nettle water through a colander into the fermentation bin.

Stir well to dissolve all the sugar, honey and malt extract. Pour in 6 pints of cold water and stir.

Check your gravity, it should be around 1040.

Add your yeast and leave to ferment for 3 weeks. Whilst a lot of recipes state much shorter times I find the beer benefits from this extended time.

Don't forget to check your final gravity, if you haven't already and want to know the percentage of alcohol in your brew.

Add a level teaspoon of sugar to each bottle and syphon the beer into the bottles. Cap the bottles (or use swing tops) and place somewhere warm for 2 days before moving to somewhere cool.

The beer should be ready to drink in 2 weeks, 3 is better.

Recipe _____

Ingredients:

Method:

Recipe

Ingredients:

Method:

Recipe

Ingredients:

Method:

Recipe

Ingredients:

Method:

It isn't as good as it's said to be,
ale, for the sons of men;
for the more a man drinks, the less he knows
about his own mind.

Non-alcoholic drinks

Whether you're pregnant, driving, or a non-drinker, the standard soft drinks can get boring. These recipes should give you some ideas for something a little more inspired.

Elderflower Cordial

For those looking for a non-alcoholic drink in the springtime, this one takes some beating. Be sure to pick your flowers on a dry day.

Serve diluted in still or sparkling water, or with lemonade.

You can also dilute 1 part cordial to 2 parts water and freeze it in lolly moulds for a lovely springtime treat.

Ingredients:

- 25 elderflower heads, in full bloom
- 4 lemons
- 500g granulated sugar
- 1.5L water (boiled)

Method:

Place the flower heads into a bucket, along with the zest and juice of the lemons.

Pour over the water, cover with a tea-towel and leave overnight.

Strain the liquid through a muslin cloth and put it into a large saucepan. Add the sugar and bring to the boil.

Pour into warm, sterilised bottles.

Refrigerate and use within a few weeks or freeze in plastic bottles for longer storage.

Drivers Mead

Do you feel left out of celebrations when you are the nominated driver, pregnant, or are too young to drink? You need this lovely non-alcoholic mead recipe. Not to be shared with drinkers!

Ingredients:

- 340g honey
- 1 litre boiled water
- Quarter teaspoon cinnamon
- Quarter teaspoon ginger
- Quarter teaspoon nutmeg
- 2 cloves
- Pinch of chilli (optional)

Method:

Put all your ingredients into a large pan and gently heat for around 10 minutes.

Strain through a muslin cloth into a clean container and refrigerate. Can be drunk straight away.

No Mojo Mojito

When Emma was pregnant, I decided she needed to be able to have a celebratory drink for her birthday. Along came this refreshing mojito recipe.

Ingredients:

- 1 tsp brown sugar
- 6 sprigs of mint
- Crushed ice
- Shot glass of apple juice
- Lemonade
- 1 lime

Method:

Put the mint and sugar into a pestle and mortar and mash together.

Half fill a glass with ice and add the mint.

Add the apple juice and top up with lemonade.

Serve with a slice of lime.

<u>**Recipe**</u>

Ingredients:

Method:

Recipe

Ingredients:

Method:

Recipe

Ingredients:

Method:

146

Further Reading

This book is only meant as a beginner's guide, so with that in mind, here are some suggested further reading. These are all books that we own and have learnt from:

The River Cottage Handbook series

Each book concentrates on a specific area and is written by an expert in that topic. There are books on bread, meat, fish, vegetables, preserves and booze, to name but a few.

An Early Meal - *Daniel Serra*

This is a well-researched book with meals 'inspired' by traditional food and includes lots of background info into the research behind it. This along with a brief chat with Daniel Serra, the author, was what made us realise we couldn't write a good 'historical meals' book.

The Meadhall - Stephen Pollington

This includes a small section on Anglo Saxon meals and drinks. Very useful in the early stages of this book.

Booze for Free - Andy Hamilton

Whilst it doesn't actually tell you how to make booze for free, it's a good guide to the basics of brewing with some nice recipes to try.

Making Mead - Brian Acton & Peter Duncan

Lots of interesting things in this very small book. A brief history and a good selection of mead recipes and melomels.

Baking Sourdough Bread - Goran Soderin & George Strachal

Great for further ideas and recipes for baking sourdough breads and making starters with ingredients other than flour.

Wild food – Roger Phillips

A great guide to foraging everything from mushrooms to flowers, and includes recipes for what to make with your findings.

Cattle die, and kinsmen die,
and so one dies one's self;
one thing I know that never dies,
the fame of a dead man's deeds.

Printed in Great
Britain
by Amazon